PATSY HOOD

The Boy From Heaven

The Forgotten Books Of The Bible - The Lost Childhood Of Jesus

First edition

ISBN (paperback): 9781969066641

ISBN (hardcover): 9781969066634

This book was professionally typeset on Reedsy.

Find out more at reedsy.com

Dedication

To my sons, James and Michael, You are my living blessings, my heart's beat, the reason I keep reaching for more. Your love and support, thinking I could write a book, means so much to me! To my beloved daughter, Jaime, My Mama and my brother, Greg, are in heaven; your spirits walk beside me always. You are in my heart forever. To my sisters, Debbie, Lucita, Diane, I'm doing this for our Mama!

My love is written into every word of these pages.

"And the child grew and became strong. He was filled with wisdom, and the grace of God was on him." (Luke 2: 40)

Before He carried the cross, He carried toys in His hands. Before He calmed the storm, He learned to walk on dirt roads. He was a child, just like us, yet still the Son of God.

Patsy Hood

TABLE OF CONTENTS

Foreword

Some readers may wonder about the moments in this book where young Jesus shows anger or power that seems frightening. I want to share my heart and faith about that! When Jesus was a child. He was still divine, the Son of God. Yet He was also growing and learning as a human boy! In the stories told in "The Infancy Gospel of Thomas", He isn't sinning or doing evil. These moments remind us that all life belongs to God alone. Jesus had the authority to give life and take it, just as His Father in Heaven does! I believe these stories show not cruelty, but the holiness of His power even when He was small. Through them we see how He grows into wisdom, mercy and love, preparing for the great sacrifice, He would one day make for all of us! I wrote this book out of a great love for Jesus to help children and grownups too, imagine what it would have been like to walk beside Him as a boy full of light, learning and the wonder of Heaven! Over 2,000 years ago, Jesus was born in a little town called Bethlehem. He grew up in a small village named Nazareth, in a land called Galilee (which is now part of Israel). Life back then was very different from today. There were no phones, no cars, no TVs, just quiet towns, dusty roads, and homes made from stone and wood. Most people were farmers, shepherds, or carpenters like Jesus' father, Joseph. Children helped with chores, played in the dusty streets, and learned stories about God from their families. The Bible tells us about Jesus' birth and a little bit about when He was twelve years old. But what about all the years in between? What could have happened? That's where this book comes in. These are stories of healing, kindness, learning, and love. They show Jesus as both a child and a miracle worker, just like only He could be. Now, you get to hear them too.

The Boy From Heaven - From the Forgotten Books of the Bible - The Lost Childhood of Jesus.

Preface

Dear Parents, we all long to teach our children about Jesus, the healer, the Savior, the Son of God. But sometimes we overlook a powerful truth, before He walked on water, He learned to walk. Before he preached to crowds, he asked simple questions. Jesus was once a child, too. These stories, drawn from the Forgotten Books of the Bible, give us a glimpse into His childhood. Though they were not included in the final version of the Bible (chosen by early church leaders to focus on salvation and doctrine), these ancient writings have survived for centuries, quietly holding precious details about His early years. So why share them now? Because children need to see that Jesus understands their world. He knows what it's like to be young, to stumble, to wonder, and to grow. These stories show them that the One who loves them so deeply has been where they are. He learned obedience, practiced kindness, made mistakes, and matured under the loving guidance of His parents. Telling these stories isn't about changing the Bible; it's about giving our children a fuller picture of the Savior, the One who came as a baby, lived as a child, and grew into the man who died for us and all we have to do is to invite him into our heart. Let these pages speak to your child's heart. Let them meet Jesus not just as Lord but as a friend who truly understands. With love and purpose, Patsy Hood

Acknowledgments

This book, The Boy from Heaven - The Forgotten Books of the Bible-The Lost Childhood of Jesus, was written by me, but it was inspired and guided by the Holy Spirit every step of the way. There were moments I didn't know what to write, times when I felt unsure, but God carried me through it. This is not just my book; it is His message, through my hands. To my sons, Michael & James, thank you, because I have two handsome & smart boys! As a mother of two boys, I've seen firsthand the energy, curiosity, and occasional mischief, and sometimes terrible mischief, lol, that come with little hearts full of life. Boys are loud, some are quiet, loving, wild, and wonderful, always climbing, exploring, and testing limits. Raising my sons gave me a window into the joy and challenge of boyhood, and helped me imagine Jesus not only as holy, but also human, a child who laughed, learned, and lived fully. Mama was the best word to me. It's what made writing this story feel real to me. I could never have done this without you. I have strived to be the best I could be for you guys! To every child who ever wondered about Jesus, to every heart that longed to know more, and to everyone who's ever felt forgotten, this story is for you. These pages hold more than ancient stories; they hold the hope and humanity of our Savior, who came as a child, lived among us, and still walks with us today. Some parents may choose to see this as a gentle, imaginative way to help children learn about Jesus, while others may accept it as a sacred manuscript that reveals parts of His childhood once left out. Either way, this is a remarkable story meant to be read, shared, and remembered. Because to know Jesus even as a boy is to know the heart of God. May this book bring light to those searching, comfort to those hurting, and joy to every heart that still believes. With all my love and gratitude, Patsy Hood

Prologue

Before He calmed the storm, healed the blind, or walked the road to the cross, Jesus was a child. He laughed. He cried. He made mistakes, learned lessons, and discovered who He was. He lived in a simple home, played in the dirt, followed His mother, and watched His earthly father work with wood. And even as the Son of God, He walked through childhood just like us, day by day, growing in spirit and strength. The Bible tells us so little about those early years. But long ago, before the books of the New Testament were chosen, stories were passed from one believer to another about the young Jesus, stories full of wonder, mystery, and truth. These stories were gathered into what we now call the Infancy Gospel of Thomas. Though not included in the Bible today, they continue to inspire questions, faith, and awe. This book is my retelling of those stories for children, families, and anyone who has ever wondered: "What was Jesus like before the world knew His name?" I've written this book with love, faith, and a heart full of miracles because I've seen what God can do. I've felt His hand in my life. I know that the same Jesus who lived as a little boy still lives today and still works wonders in the hearts of those who believe. Come with me now, and step into the quiet streets of Nazareth, where a young boy named Jesus is just beginning His story. This is the story of a child who

was fully human, fully divine, and full of heavenly purpose.

This is the forgotten childhood of Jesus. This is "The Boy from Heaven."

Patsy Hood

Introduction

For generations, we have heard the story of Jesus' birth in Bethlehem, His miracles, and His sacrifice on the cross. Yet there is a part of His life that remains little known, the years of His childhood. What was Jesus like as a boy? How did He grow, play, and learn? What did people see in Him before His public ministry began? The stories you are about to read come from an ancient text known as The Infancy Gospel of Thomas. This book, written nearly two thousand years ago, was not included in the Bible we read today, yet it preserves a glimpse of Jesus as a child. Though not part of Scripture, these stories invite us to imagine the boyhood of the Savior with wonder and reverence. In The Boy From Heaven, I have retold these stories with simplicity and warmth for children and families. My hope is that each chapter will open a window into Jesus' early life, moments of joy, challenge, and divine power that remind us that God's presence was with Him from the very beginning. 1 This book is not meant to replace the Holy Bible, but to spark curiosity, inspire faith, and help us see Jesus in a new and tender way as both fully God and fully human, who once walked this earth as a little boy. May you be blessed as you read, and may these pages draw you closer to the heart of the One who came down from heaven for us all.

Patsy Hood

Chapter 1

Birth of Jesus

In Nazareth , there lived a young woman named Mary . She was kind and full of love . One day, something very special happened, and an angel named Gabriel visited her in the blaze of heavenly light with wonderful news. "Mary," the angel said, "you will have a baby. He will be the Son of God sent to save the whole world." Mary believed the angel and soon, just as the angel said, she was going to have a baby. Not long after, the emperor of the land, Augustus, made a big announcement. Everyone had to travel back to their family's hometown to be counted. So, Joseph, Mary's husband, gently helped her onto a donkey, and they began their journey to Bethlehem, the city where Joseph's family came from. But as the sun began to set and they passed a quiet hillside cave, Mary knew the time had come. "Joseph," shesaidsoftly, "I can't go any farther . The baby is coming . Please , let's stop here ." Joseph looked around and saw the small , cool cave . " Rest here , Mary , " he said . "I will find help." Joseph hurried off toward the town and found an old woman from Jerusalem walking along the road. "Please, kind woman," Joseph said, "come with me. My wife is about to give birth, and she needs help!" The woman followed Joseph as quickly as her feet would go. By the time they reached the cave, the sun had gone down. But something wonderful happened, inside the cave, it was brighter than day. A holy light filled the room, shining even brighter than lamps, candles, or the sun itself. There, wrapped in swaddling cloth, baby Jesus rested peacefully in Mary 's arms, gently drinking her milk. The old woman's eyes grew wide. She had never seen anything like this. She turned to Mary and asked, "Are you truly the mother of this child?" Mary smiled gently and said, "Yes, I am." The old woman said, "You are not like other women." And Mary replied, "Just as there is no child like my son, there is no mother like me." Then something even more special happened; this woman had been suffering for a long time. She was filled with darkness. Satan himself had taken hold of her.

Every night, she ran through the streets, tearing at her clothes and shouting. People tried to tie her with ropes and chains, but she broke free and ran wild into the hills or stood in graveyards, throwing stones at strangers. "From this day on," she said, "I will serve this child with all my heart."

That night, some shepherds were nearby, watching over their sheep. When they heard about the birth of the holy baby, they hurried to the cave. They made a fire and sang songs of joy! Their voices rang out in music, praising God. The cave glowed like a golden temple, filled with songs from heaven and earth, all singing together: "Glory to God! The Savior is born!" The old woman fell to her knees and lifted her hands in praise of the Lord, "God of Israel," she said, "Thank You for letting me see this miracle, the birth of the Savior of the world!" And so, in a quiet cave beneath the stars, with angels singing and hearts rejoicing, the Son of God came into the world, born in a manger, not in a palace, but in the arms of a loving mother and surrounded by the prayers of the humble. Jesus, the boy from Heaven, has come!

Chapter 2

The Light in The Temple

Eight days after baby Jesus was born, Mary and Joseph followed the law of God and had Him circumcised. Still resting in the quiet cave, they held the sacred ceremony there, wrapped in peace and love. An old Hebrew woman who had helped care for baby Jesus took something sacred from that day, some say it was His tiny foreskin, others say it was the cord that once connected Him to His mother, and gently placed it inside a beautiful alabaster box. The box was filled with sweet-smelling oil called spikenard; a treasure saved for something holy. She told her son, who was a seller of oils and perfumes, "Guard this box with your life. Even if someone offers you a fortune, three hundred silver coins, never sell it."

Years later, a woman with a sorrowful heart would pour that same sweet oil onto Jesus' head and feet, wiping it away with her hair as a sign of her love.

When Jesus was just 40 days old, Mary and Joseph took Him to the great temple in Jerusalem, as the law of Moses had taught. The city's streets were crowded with travelers, but in Mary's arms, the tiny Child rested peacefully, unaware of the great prophecy soon to be spoken over Him. There, they offered two small birds as a gift to God because every firstborn son was to be dedicated as holy to the Lord. But when Mary carried baby Jesus into the temple, something incredible happened. Suddenly, a heavenly light surrounded Him. It shone from Him like a golden pillar of light, reaching up toward heaven. Everyone around paused and stared in wonder. Angels gathered all around Him, gentle, glowing beings with wings as soft as feathers and eyes filled with joy. They stood tall and still, like royal guards around a little King.

Among the people in the temple was an old man named Simeon. He had waited his whole life for this moment. God had promised him that he would not die until he saw the Savior of the world with his own eyes. When Simeon saw Jesus glowing in Mary's arms, he walked toward them, his hands reaching out with trembling joy. He looked up to heaven and said softly: "Lord, now I can go in peace. My eyes have seen Your light, the Savior You promised, a light to shine for all people, and the glory of Israel!" And nearby was a kind and wise prophetess named Hannah. She, too, saw the baby that night, some shepherds were nearby, watching over their sheep.

When they heard about the birth of the holy baby, they hurried to the cave. They made a fire and sang songs of joy! Their voices rang out in music, praising God. The cave glowed like a golden temple, filled with songs from heaven and earth, all singing together: "Glory to God! The Savior is born!" The woman fell to her knees and lifted her hands in praise of the Lord, "God of Israel," she said, "Thank You for letting me see this miracle, the birth of the Savior of the world!" And so, in a quiet cave beneath the stars, with angels singing and hearts rejoicing, the Son of God came into the world, born in a manger, not in a palace, but in the arms of a loving mother and surrounded by the prayers of the humble. Jesus, the boy from Heaven, has come.

Chapter 3

The Wise Men and the Gift from Mary

Baby Jesus was born in Bethlehem, during the time of King Herod, Herod was an evil man, these wise men were supposed to return and tell him where baby Jesus was because King Herod feared the baby Jesus was going to take over his throne. They read an old prophecy and followed a bright star that led them right to Jesus. They brought Him special gifts, shining gold, sweet smelling frankincense, and myrrh, and they bowed down to worship Him. Mary, the mother of Jesus, wanted to give them something, too. She took one of the soft swaddling clothes she had wrapped Jesus in and gave it to them as a gift. The wise men were so thankful and knew it was a very precious present. As they left, the same bright light that an angel in the form of a star appeared to guide them safely home. The wise men did not go back and tell the King where

Jesus was, instead they went home. When they returned, their own kings and princes asked them about the journey. The wise men showed them the cloth from Mary. In their land, it was a custom to honor special things by placing them in a fire.

They gently laid the cloth in the flames, but to their amazement, the fire did not burn it at all! When they took it out, it was as perfect as before. It remained untouched. They kissed the swaddling cloth, placed it on their heads and eyes with great respect, and said, "This is a true and wonderful thing." They whispered to one another. Then they placed it carefully among their treasures, to keep it safe forever.

Chapter 4

The Stay in Egypt

King Herod made a degree that all babies, two and under were to be killed, because he wanted to make sure Jesus didn't live. Herod could not tolerate the thought of another king being born, even a newborn! An angel appeared to Joseph in a dream and told him to flee to Egypt with Mary and Jesus. The family journeyed onward to Memphis, a city in Egypt, where they met Pharaoh and stayed for three years. During that time, young Jesus performed many miracles, so many that not even the books written about His childhood could record them all. He healed the sick, comforted the hurting, and showed love to everyone.

Chapter 5

Miracles On the Road

Joseph and Mary, with little Jesus in Mary's arms, continued traveling from city to city. Everywhere they went, amazing things happened because wherever Jesus was love and healing followed. Crowds gathered and followed His gentle light.

Later that day, they entered a new town where a wedding was about to take place. But something was wrong. The bride could not speak Some said that she had been cursed by wicked sorcerers. Then, as Mary walked into town carrying baby Jesus, the bride saw them. She ran to Mary, gently took Jesus in her arms, and hugged Him close, kissing Him again and again. At that moment, her voice returned Her ears opened, and she began to sing songs of joy and praise to God. That night, the whole town celebrated, not just the wedding, but the miracle. Laughter and music filled the town. They said, "Surely God and His angels have come to visit us.

The Girl with Leprosy

There was a girl who had a terrible skin disease called leprosy. Her skin was white and rough, and no one could cure her. People avoided her, stepping aside when she passed. The woman took the water she had used to bathe Jesus and sprinkled it on the girl. And right before their eyes, the leprosy disappeared! Her skin became soft and clean. The people were amazed. They whispered to one another, "Joseph, Mary, and this baby. They must be more than just travelers. They must be from Heaven." The girl, now healed didn't want to leave them. "Please," she asked, "May I go with you?" Mary and Joseph agreed, and she joyfully joined them on their journey.

Chapter 6

The Mule and The Wedding

They came afterwards to another city and had a mind to lodge there. So, they went to a man's house, who was newly married, but due to the influence of sorcerers, he was 't able to be with his wife. While they were lodging at his house that night the man was freed from his disorder. When they were preparing early in the morning to go forward on their journey, the newly married person stopped them and provided a noble entertainment for them. Continuing on the next day, they came to another city, and saw three women coming from a certain grave with great weeping. When Mary saw them, she spoke to the girl who was their companion, saying "Go and ask them what is the matter with them, and what misfortune has befallen them?" When the girl asked them, they gave her no answer, but asked her, "Who are you, and where are you going?" "For the day is far spent and the night is at hand , " Come along with us, and lodge with us ."They then followed them and were brought into a new house , well furnished with all sorts of furniture .

It was wintertime, and the girl went into the parlor where these women were and found them weeping and lamenting, as before. By them stood a mule, covered with silk, and an ebony collar hanging down from its neck, which they kissed and were feeding. But when the girl said, "How handsome that mule is, ladies!" They replied with tears and said, "This mule, which you see, was our brother, born of the same mother as we. When our father died and left us a very large estate, we had only this brother. We endeavored to find him a suitable match and thought he should be married like other men, but some giddy and jealous woman bewitched him without our knowledge. One night, just before dawn, while all the doors of the house were securely shut, we saw that our brother had been changed into a mule, just as you now see him.

"We, as sad as you see us now," having no father to comfort us, have appealed to all the wise men, magicians, and diviners in the world, but they have been of no service to us. As often as we find ourselves oppressed with grief, we rise and go with our mother to our father's tomb, where, after we have cried enough, we return home." When the girl had heard this, she said,

"Take courage, and cease your fears, for a remedy for your afflictions is near at hand, among you, even in the midst of your house. For I was also leprous

; but when I saw this woman and this little infant with her, whose name is Jesus, I sprinkled my body with the water with which his mother had washed him, and I was immediately made well. I am certain that he is also capable of relieving you from your distress. Wherefore, arise, go to my mistress, Mary, and when you have brought her into your own parlor, disclose to her the secret; at the same time, be open and honest." As soon as the women heard the girl's words, they hastened away to Mary, introduced themselves to her, and, sitting down before her, they wept and said, Mary, pity your handmaids, for we have no head of our family, no one older than us; no father or brother to go in and out before us. But this mule, which you see, is our brother, whom some woman, through witchcraft, has brought into this condition you see now. We therefore ask for understanding!" Then, Mary was grieved at their case. She took the Lord Jesus and put him on the back of the mule. And said to her son, "Oh Jesus Christ, restore this mule and grant him again the shape of a man and rational creature as before!" This was scarcely said by Mary, the mule immediately changed into a human form, and became a young man without any deformity.

Then he, and his mother, and the sisters worshiped Mary, and lifting the child upon their heads, they kissed him and said, "Blessed is your mother, O Jesus, O Savior of the world! Blessed are the eyes that are fortunate enough to see you." Then both sisters told their mother, "Truly, our brother has been restored to his former shape by the help of the Lord Jesus Christ and the kindness of the girl who told us about Mary and her son. Since our brother is unmarried, it is only right that we marry him to this girl, their servant."

When they consulted Mary about this matter, and she had given her consent, they arranged a splendid wedding for the girl. And so, their sorrow being turned into gladness, and their mourning into happiness, they began to rejoice, make merry, and sing, dressed in their richest attire, with bracelets. Afterwards, they glorified and praised God, saying, "O Jesus, Son of David, who changes sorrow into gladness and mourning into happiness!" After this, Joseph and Mary stayed there for ten days, then went away, having received great respect from the people. When they took their leave and returned home, the people cried, especially the girl.

Chapter 7

The Way Back Home

After living safely in Egypt for a while, Joseph and Mary heard some very strange and frightening news. A great idol, one of the statues the Egyptians worshiped, had suddenly fallen and shattered into pieces! People said it happened just because baby Jesus had walked by. Joseph and Mary looked at one another with wide, worried eyes. "When we were in Israel," Joseph said softly, "King Herod tried to kill Jesus. He even sent soldiers to hurt the babies in Bethlehem. What if the people here grow angry and blame Jesus for the idol falling?" Mary nodded, holding baby Jesus close to her chest. "They might try to burn us with fire. We must leave this place."

So, under the stars and through the wild hills, they began their journey back toward home. The road was not easy.

One night, they came to a dangerous place, deep in the hills where robbers hid. Robbers were known for attacking travelers. They stole their belongings, tied them up, and left them helpless. No one dared come near. But Joseph and Mary had no other path to take. With courage and prayer in their hearts, they stepped forward.

Then something incredible happened. As the Holy Family approached the thieves' hideout, a mighty sound filled the air. It wasn't from people, or horses, or wagons. It came from Heaven. It sounded like a king's parade marching from a shining city. Horses galloping, golden trumpets playing, and an army too big to count, rode through the skies. The robbers were terrified. They looked around wildly, their faces pale with fear. "What is that sound?" one shouted in fear. "Who is coming?" cried another. "Run!" they all screamed, dropping everything they had stolen and fleeing into the shadows. Left behind were the poor travelers, whom the robbers had captured, tied up, and scared. But now, hearing the sound of freedom in the air, the prisoners sat up, looked around, and slowly unwrapped the ropes from their hands. They stood, stretched, and each one took back what had been stolen from him.

Just then, they saw Joseph, Mary, and baby Jesus coming down the road. "Wait!" the people called. "Where is the king whose army came before Him? The one the robbers heard? He saved us!"

Joseph looked at them with kind eyes and said gently, "He will come after us." And they didn't understand it then, but one day, that child in Mary's arms would come not with an army of horses, but with an army of love. He would set prisoners free, not with swords, but with truth and mercy. So, the family walked on, the hidden King held safely in His mother's arms, and the hills behind them whispered songs of wonder.

The King with No Throne

Ins 't it amazing that the Lord of all the lands, the King of Heaven, had no golden throne, no crown of jewels, no army or palace? Instead, He was carried gently from town to town, through deserts and danger, wrapped in His mother's arms. But wherever He went, miracles bloomed and hearts were healed, because He was the King of Love.

Chapter 8

The Kind Robber and the Secret Spring

As they journeyed through distant lands, Joseph, Mary, and the little child

Jesus came to a wide and lonely desert. People warned them, "Don't go that way, robbers hide in those hills!" So, Joseph and Mary decided to travel quietly at night, under the stars, trusting that God would protect them.

The Sleeping Robbers

As they walked carefully through the darkness, they saw something ahead in the road, two men fast asleep, with a gang of other robbers snoring beside them. These two were known by the names Titus and Dumachus . Titus woke up and noticed Joseph, Mary, and baby Jesus coming close. He whispered to Dumachus , "Please let this little family pass by . Don't wake the others . Let no harm come to them ." But Dumachus frowned . "Why should we let them go ? " Titus replied, "I will give you forty silver coins and even my own belt as a promise, just don't make a sound. Let them go in peace."

A Blessing for the Kind Robber

Mary saw what Titus had done. Her eyes filled with gratitude. She said softly, "May the Lord God receive you kindly, may He forgive your sins and bless you forever." Then little Jesus, though only a child, looked up and said something amazing to His mother, "Mother, many years from now, when I am thirty-three, the people in Jerusalem will hang me on a cross. These two robbers, Titus and Dumachus, will be with me. Titus on my right and Dumachus on my left. Titus, who was kind tonight, will enter Paradise with me." Mary's heart grew heavy. "God forbid that this should ever happen to you, my son," she whispered. And yet, deep down, she knew her child was born to save the world, true God in human form. As the Holy Family approached the next city, something powerful happened; the city crumbled into sand dunes, the idols fell, and all was silent. The people had no words, for they had never seen such power before.

Chapter 9

The Tree That Gave Water

Not far from that place was a large, beautiful sycamore tree, in a place now called Matara. Under that tree, Jesus caused a spring of water to burst from the ground! Mary bent down and gently washed her little boy's coat in the cool water. Where his tiny drops of sweat had fallen near the tree, a sweet-smelling balsam plant began to grow. People would one day say, "This tree is blessed by Heaven!"

Chapter 10

Caleb and the Wicked Woman

One of the towns the Holy Family traveled thur lived two women in the same house . They were both married to the same man, and each had a little boy. One woman was named Mary, and her son was named Caleb. Caleb was very sick. One day, Caleb's mother walked to the home of Mary, the mother of Jesus. She carried a beautiful, handmade carpet. "Please, Mary," she said kindly, "Accept this gift and give me a piece of your baby Jesus' swaddling cloth for my son." Mary smiled warmly, accepted the gift, and gave her a small piece of Jesus' cloth. Later that night, Caleb's mother made a tiny coat from the cloth and wrapped Caleb in it. Right away, his fever went away. Miraculously, he was laughing and playing again! The other woman's son did not get better. He grew weaker and, sadly, passed away. This was the First Miracle. One day, when it was Caleb's mother's turn to bake bread, she was heating the oven. She went to fetch the flour, leaving Caleb nearby. The jealous woman saw the boy alone. Her eyes burned with anger. Quietly, she took little Caleb and pushed him into the hot oven. She ran away quickly, thinking no one would ever know. When Caleb's mother returned and opened the oven door, she gasped. There was Caleb, safe and smiling. The oven was cold as snow. She ran to Mary in tears. "Look what my neighbor has done." "Shhh" said Mary gently. "Let's not tell others yet. God sees everything."

A few days later, Caleb was playing near a well when the jealous woman saw him again. This time, she crept up behind him and pushed him into the deep water. But God was watching. Some men came to draw water and saw the little boy sitting calmly on top of the water, as if it were solid ground. They pulled him out with ropes and were amazed. They praised God for protecting this special boy. Again, Caleb's mother ran to Mary. "Please, she will harm him again. I fear for his life!" Mary looked at her with kind eyes. "Do not worry. God will protect the innocent."

Justice From Heaven

One morning, the jealous woman went to fetch water. As she pulled on the rope, her foot became tangled. She tripped and fell headfirst into the well. Her head was badly injured, and she did not survive. And so, the old saying came true: "They dig a deep well for others, but fall into it themselves."

Chapter 11

The Boy Called Bartholomew

In the same town, another mother had two little boys. Sadly, one had just passed away, and the other was very sick and close to death. She carried him in her arms to Mary, tears running down her cheeks. "Mary, please help me!" she cried. "I had two sons. One I have already lost to death! Please pray that God lets me keep this one." Mary saw her sorrow and said gently, "Lay him in Jesus' bed, and cover him with His little blanket." The mother did as she was told. As soon as the dying boy touched the bed and the clothes of baby Jesus, something wonderful happened. His eyes opened wide. He sat up and smiled. "Mommy, I'm hungry!" he said, reaching out for food. The mother wept with joy and whispered, "Now I know the power of God lives in your son, Mary." This boy would grow up to be called Bartholomew, one of the twelve disciples of Jesus.

Chapter 12

The Healing Water of Jesus

The Princess Secret

There was a woman whose skin was covered in painful spots. She was very sick with leprosy and didn't know what to do. One day, she heard about a kind woman named Mary and her little boy named Jesus. The woman came to Mary and cried, "O kind Lady, please help me."

Mary gently replied, "Do you need gold or silver, or do you want to be healed?" The woman said, "Who could ever heal me?" Mary smiled softly. "Wait just a moment," she said. "Let me bathe my son and put him to bed" When baby Jesus was tucked in, Mary gave the woman the water she had used to gently wash Him. "Take this water and pour it over your skin," she said. The woman did as Mary instructed, and instantly, her skin became clean. She was healed, just like that. She thanked God with all her heart. She stayed with Mary for three days, learning and rejoicing. When she returned to her town, she saw something very sad. A young princess stood nearby, crying with her family. The girl had a small white mark between her eyes, the first sign of leprosy. Her husband, a prince, had ended their marriage because he feared the illness would spread. The woman gently asked, "Why are you so sad?" The princess's family didn't want to talk at first, but the woman kindly insisted. "Please tell me. I was once sick too, but I found healing"

So, they told her the story, and she said, "Come with me. I know someone who can help!" Together, they gathered special gifts and traveled to find Mary, the mother of Jesus, Mary greeted them with love and said, "May the mercy of the Lord Jesus be upon you." She gave them water she had used to wash baby Jesus. "Wash with this water" she said. They did, and immediately the young princess was healed. Her skin became clear, and her tears turned into joy. Everyone praised God. They sang songs of thanksgiving and returned home filled with happiness. The prince, hearing his wife had been healed, ran to her and hugged her. They were married once more, and this time with even more love and thankfulness in their hearts.

Chapter 13

The Girl and the Dragon of Darkness

In Bethlehem there lived a girl who was very ill. A wicked spirit would visit her, sometimes as a terrifying dragon. He drained her strength and left her weak and pale. She would cry out, "Oh, who will help me? Please, someone, stop this dragon!" Her parents wept and held her close, but they didn't know what to do. One day, the princess who had been healed of leprosy heard about the girl. She climbed to the top of her palace and saw her crying with her hands around her head. The princess sent for the girl's mother. "Tell me your daughter's story," she said. "I was healed by a woman named Mary, the mother of Jesus. Maybe she can help your daughter, too." The mother felt hope raised in her heart. She packed quickly and traveled with her daughter all the way to Bethlehem. They found Mary and told her everything. Mary listened with kindness and said, "Take this water. I washed my son Jesus with it. Pour it over your daughter's body." She also handed the mother a soft cloth made from Jesus' swaddling clothes. "When you see the dragon," she said, "Hold this cloth up. God will protect you." Show him, the cloth." As the dragon came near, the girl bravely held the cloth to her face. Suddenly, WHOOSH! Flames burst from the cloth like fire from Heaven. The dragon cried out, "Ahh! What have I to do with you, Jesus, Son of Mary?" He was terrified and ran away, never to return again. The girl was finally free. She sang songs of joy and thanked God. Everyone who saw this miracle gave praise to God, for they had witnessed His power and love through the child Jesus.

Chapter 14

The Boy with The Anger Spirit

A woman lived with her little boy named Judas. He wasn't like other children. Sometimes, something dark and scary would take over his heart, making him do strange and hurtful things. He would growl like a wild animal, bite anyone nearby, and if no one was close, he'd bite his own hands in sadness. This poor mother wept every day. She had tried everything. One day, she heard about Mary and her child, Jesus, how He was kind and full of God's power. With hope in her heart, she carried Judas through the village and up to where Jesus was playing with His cousins, James and Jose. The children were laughing and running when Judas walked up and sat beside Jesus. Suddenly, his face changed. That dark spirit came over him again. Judas tried to bite Jesus. But he couldn't. So instead, he hit Jesus hard on the side. Jesus cried out, but in that very moment, the angry spirit flew out of Judas like a wild dog, running away madly. Judas blinked and looked around, free, quiet, calm for the very first time.

Little did anyone know that this boy, Judas, would one day be His disciple and grow up to betray our Lord with a kiss! And the side where he struck Jesus would be the same side pierced when Jesus gave his life for all of us.

Chapter 15

The Clay Birds and the Miracle Dyer

When Jesus was seven years old, He loved playing with the other children in town. One sunny day, they sat in the sand and shaped clay into animals, donkeys, cows, birds, and other little creatures. Each child smiled proudly, showing off their creation. Then Jesus said softly, "Would you like to see mine come to life?" Suddenly, they began to move. The donkeys trotted, the cows nodded, and the birds flapped their wings and flew high into the air. Some even flew down to nibble on seeds or sip water from a tiny dish Jesus made for them. The boys cheered, but when they ran home and told their parents, the grown-ups didn't understand. They thought He was **dangerous,** a boy with a power no one could explain, and they feared what might happen if their children stayed too close to Him.

One afternoon, as Jesus walked past a shop where cloth was dyed in bright colors, he saw that the dyer, a man named Salem, had stepped out. Jesus peeked inside and saw stacks of cloth ready to be dyed. With a playful idea, Jesus tossed every piece into the hot dye pot! When Salem returned, he gasped in horror. "Oh no! You've ruined everything! These were all to be dyed different colors for the people." Jesus smiled gently. "Don't worry. Watch this." He reached into the pot and pulled out each piece of cloth. Amazingly, each one was dyed exactly the right color, just as Salem's customers had asked for reds, blues, greens, and golds. Salem's eyes filled with tears. "This is a miracle!" he whispered. When the townspeople saw, they began to praise God too.

Chapter 16

The Bed That Was Too Small

Joseph, Jesus'earthlyfather, was carpenter. He worked hard building things like doors, stools, shelves, and tables. He wasn't the best with measurements, but thankfully, little Jesus often helped him. When something needed to be longer or shorter, Jesus would stretch out His tiny hand and poo! The wood would become exactly the right size. One day, the King of Jerusalem sent for Joseph. "I want you to build me a beautiful bed," the King said. "It must fit perfectly in my royal bed chamber." Joseph worked day and night for two years building the bed. It was made from special wood like King Solomon had used, carved with beautiful shapes and swirls. But when Joseph placed the bed in the royal room, it was too small, two whole hand lengths short on each side. The king was furious. Joseph trembled in fear and couldn't even eat dinner "I've failed," he whispered sadly. Jesus sat beside him and gently took his hand. "Don't be afraid, Papa. God is with us. Just do what I say" Then Jesus said, "You pull one side, and I'll pull the other." As they pulled, the bed stretched before their eyes, growing just enough to fit the space perfectly. The king and all his helpers gasped. "It's a miracle!" they said. They all praised God for the child who worked beside his father and made everything just right.

Chapter 17

The Hiding Game and the Shepherd's Call

One sunny afternoon, little Jesus saw a group of children playing hide and seek. With a joyful heart, He ran to join them. But as soon as the children saw Him, they giggled and scattered, hiding in all directions. Jesus knocked on a nearby door where some woman stood. "Have you seen the boys?" He asked. "There's no one here," the woman replied. Jesus looked kindly at them and pointed to a furnace behind the house. "Then who are those kids in there?" Peeking inside, the woman gasped. "Why, those are just little goats!" Jesus smiled and called out, "Come out, little kids, your shepherd is here!" At once, the goats leapt out and turned back into the boys. They danced and laughed around Jesus. The woman fell to her knees. "O Lord Jesus, Son of Mary, you are truly the good shepherd of Israel!" Jesus gently raised them and said, "Come, children. Let us go play once more." The boys, happily restored, skipped after Him into the sunlight.

Chapter 18

The Flower King and the Serpent's Secret

During the month of February or March, Jesus gathered His friends and made Himself a pretend king. The children spread their cloaks on the ground and placed a crown of flowers on His head. Some stood like royal guards. Anyone passing by was kindly asked, "Come, bow before the King for a safe journey!

" While they played, a group of men approached, carrying a boy on a blanket. The boy had been bitten by a poisonous serpent while gathering wood. Seeing the "king," the men tried to pass quietly, but the children ran up to them "Come see the King!" they said. The men didn't want to stop, but the boys gently pulled them along Jesus stood and asked, "Why are you carrying this boy?" "He was bitten by a serpent, "they said. "He is very sick" "Let's go find the serpent," Jesus said. The parents hesitated, but the boys insisted, "Didn't the King speak? We must go ! "

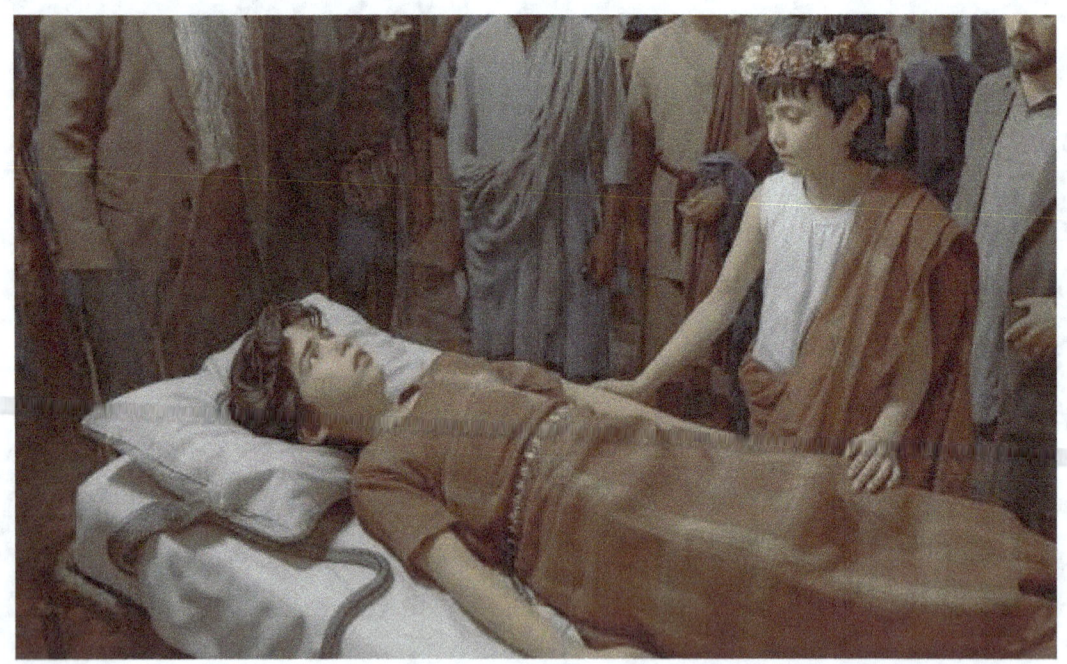

So, they returned to the place where the serpent had struck. Jesus pointed to the nest and called, "Come here, serpent!" The snake slithered out and bowed before Him. "Take back the poison from the boy," Jesus said. The serpent obeyed and gently drew out the poison. Then Jesus said, "Now be gone." The serpent burst apart Jesus touched the boy's hand and he awoke, healthy again. "Do not cry" Jesus said. "One day, you will be my disciple." And that boy grew up to be Simon the Canaanite, one of Jesus' closest friends.

Another day, the boys were playing on a rooftop when one boy fell and died.

Everyone ran away, except Jesus. The boy's family came and blamed Jesus. "You pushed him!" "I did not," Jesus said calmly. "Ask him yourself." He knelt beside the boy and called, "Zenanas, who pushed you?" The boy opened his eyes and said, "Not Jesus, another boy did." Everyone was amazed and praised God!

Chapter 19

Miracles and Mischief

One day as Jesus and His brother James went to gather wood. James was bitten by a viper and cried out in pain; James was terrified. Jesus quickly bent down, blew on the bite, and James was healed instantly. Now who can have a better brother than that?

The Boy Who Taught the Teachers

A schoolmaster named Zacchaeus said to Joseph, "Send Jesus to me so I can teach Him the alphabet!" So, they brought Jesus, and the teacher said, "Say Aleph." Jesus said, "First tell me what Aleph means, and then I'll say Beth." The teacher grew angry, but Jesus began to explain the meaning of each letter, how some were straight, some bent, some dotted, and why they were ordered so. The teacher was stunned. "This boy knows more than I do." They then took Jesus to an even stricter teacher. Again, Jesus said, "Tell me what Aleph means." The teacher raised his hand to strike Him, but his hand froze and withered, and he fell down dead. "This frightened Joseph, and he said to Mary, 'We really didn't know how to handle Jesus. No more school. Let's keep Him home from now on.'"

The Broken Jar

One day, Mary needing water asked Jesus to fetch some water. On His way back, the jar broke. So, Jesus gathered the water in His cloak, as if it were a bowl, and carried it home without spilling a drop!

One day on a Sabbath, Jesus and His friends made little pools on the riverbank. Jesus sculpted twelve sparrows from clay and set them around His pool. But a boy named Hanani came by and destroyed their work, shouting, "No work on the Sabbath!" Jesus clapped His hands, and the clay birds flew away chirping. When Hanani tried to destroy Jesus' pool, the water vanished. Jesus was upset and He said, "As the water disappeared, so shall your life." And the boy fell and died.

Later, a boy ran into Jesus roughly. Jesus said, "As you knocked Me down, so you will fall and not rise." The boy collapsed and did not get up. Joseph told Mary again, not knowing how to deal with Jesus' behavior "Let's keep

Jesus' home. Anyone who angers Him ends up dead."

Chapter 20

The Wonder of the Temple

"Where Is Jesus?" Jesus was now twelve years old, growing strong. Every year, Mary and Joseph made a long journey to the city of Jerusalem to celebrate the Passover Festival, just as God's people had done for generations. This year, Jesus went with them, traveling with many families and friends along the dusty roads. The festival was full of joy, singing, prayers and stories of how God had rescued His people long ago. When it ended, everyone packed up to go home. Mary and Joseph thought Jesus was walking with the others, maybe playing with His cousins or chatting with neighbors. But as the sun began to set, they looked around, and Jesus was nowhere to be found. Worried, they searched among the traveler. "Have you seen Jesus?" Mary asked one group. "Not since this morning," someone replied. Joseph's heart pounded.

"We must go back," he said. Back to Jerusalem, they hurried, retracing their steps, searching street by street, asking everyone they saw. One day passed.

Then two.

On the third day, they walked into the Temple, the great house of God. And there was Jesus He was sitting quietly among the teachers and elders, men with gray beards and scrolls in their hands. Jesus was listening carefully, asking thoughtful questions, and even answering theirs with wisdom far beyond His years. Everyone was amazed. "Who is this boy?" they whispered "How can a child understand so much?"

Mary rushed to Him and wrapped her arms around Him. "Oh, Jesus," she said with tears in her eyes, "Why did you do this to us? We've been so worried. We searched everywhere for you!" Jesus looked up with calm eyes and said, "Why were you looking for me? Didn't you know I would be in my father's house?" Some of the teachers turned to Mary. "Are you the mother of this child?" they asked "I am," she replied softly. "You, more than any woman, are truly blessed!" they said "God has filled your child with glory, wisdom, and goodness. We have never seen anything like this." Jesus stood up and gently walked beside Mary and Joseph. He went home with them and was loving and obedient, just as always. Mary treasured all these things deep in her heart. And Jesus grew stronger, wiser, and more loved by everyone around Him. To Him be glory forever and ever. Amen.

Chapter 21

Leaving Childhood Behind

As the seasons passed, Jesus grew taller and stronger. He was no longer a little boy who acted quickly out of feelings, but a child learning patience and gentleness. Mary and Joseph guided Him with love. When He wanted to run ahead, they reminded Him to wait. When His words came too sharply, they taught Him to speak with kindness. Slowly, Jesus learned the beauty of self-control, and the people of Nazareth began to notice. "See how gentle He has become," some whispered. "This boy is different." Though the

Gospel does not tell us every detail of these years, we know this, God's Spirit was shaping His Son. Day by day, Jesus was preparing for the wisdom and goodness that would amaze even the teachers in the Temple. That is how it also is with us, His children, He shapes us day by day.

Chapter 22

Jesus Is Baptized

One bright day, Jesus came to the Jordan River, where many people had gathered. At the edge of the water stood John the Baptist, a man chosen by God to prepare the way for the Savior. He was baptizing people, helping them turn their hearts back to God. When John saw Jesus' walking toward him, his heart trembled with awe. Jesus stepped into the water and said, "John, I want you to baptize Me." John was shocked. He shook his head and said, "Lord, I'm the one who should be baptized by You! And yet you're asking me?

" Jesus smiled gently and replied, "Let it be this way for now. This is part of God's plan; it's the right thing to do." John understood, and with great care, he lowered Jesus into the river. As Jesus came up from the water, the skies opened wide. A beautiful light shone down, and the Spirit of God came like a dove, resting gently on Jesus. A voice from Heaven said: "This is My beloved Son, and I am very pleased with Him." Everyone nearby stood in awe. And from that moment on, Jesus' journey of love, healing, and truth began.

2

Conclusion

And so, the boy from heaven grew.

The child who shaped birds from clay, who spoke with wisdom beyond His years, and who sometimes startled the world with His power began to walk more quietly now. His hands still worked with care. His eyes still held mystery.

But His heart grew deeper in kindness, patience, and understanding.

Those who once feared Him slowly learned to trust Him. Those who questioned Him began to listen. Mary treasured every moment, every question, every miracle, holding them close in her heart. Joseph guided Him with steady hands, teaching Him how to work, how to wait, and how to live among others

with humility.

Jesus learned obedience not because He lacked power, but because love chooses patience. Though heaven lived within Him, He chose to grow as all children do: step by step, day by day, under the sun of Nazareth.

The stories of His childhood fade here, but His journey does not end.

The boy would become a teacher.

The teacher would become a healer.

The healer would become a savior.

And yet, He would always remember what it meant to be a child small, curious, misunderstood, and deeply loved.

For the boy from heaven did not come to rule through fear, but to teach the world how love begins.

Quietly.

Gently.

As a child.

Epilogue

The Boy from Heaven: The Forgotten Childhood of Jesus Jesus was never just an ordinary child. He was the Son of God, full of power and purpose, yet He walked through childhood just like we do. He learned. He made mistakes. He grew in love and wisdom. He showed kindness. He forgave. He healed. He listened. These stories remind us that Jesus understands us because He lived as one of us. He wasn't just our Savior on the cross. He was once a little boy, too. As you close this book, I pray you remember that Jesus is still alive. He still works miracles. He still sees your heart. And He still loves you. If you've ever felt small, or unsure of your purpose, know this! Jesus once walked in your shoes. He knows the way forward. And He is always near. These stories may have been forgotten by many, but they are alive again in your heart now. Let them bring you closer to Him. Let them remind you that you are never alone. With all my love,

Patsy Hood

Afterword

The Boy from Heaven: The Forgotten Childhood of Jesus Writing this book has been a journey of faith for me. These stories reached deep into my heart, and I believe they were meant to be shared. I didn't write this as a Bible scholar. I have read "Forgotten Books Of The Bible twice. All the stories got to me, though Jesus 's life really got to me!" I could not believe this would be left out, so I wrote this as a believer, a mother, and someone who has seen the power of God at work in real life. I know miracles are real. I have lived through them. I have seen bills paid when I had nothing. My crippled arm was healed. I have seen God show up again and again, just when I needed Him most. That is why I believe these stories. Jesus was both fully God and fully human. He was a child who carried heaven inside Him. I hope that this book opens your heart to a deeper love for Jesus. Not just the man who walked on water, but the boy who ran through the streets of Nazareth. The boy who felt what we feel. The boy who knew what it was like to grow, to stumble, to forgive, and to shine with God's light. Thank you for reading. Thank you for believing. With all my heart, Patsy Hood

About the Author

Patsy Hood is an aspiring writer with a heart full of stories and a soul anchored in faith. Living in Alabama, she finds her greatest joy in sharing love, healing, and hope through the power of storytelling. The Boy from Heaven is her first published children's book, inspired by her deep desire to help children see the gentleness, wonder, and divine calling in the childhood of Jesus. She believes every child should know the story of Jesus as a child!

Also, by Patsy Hood

I write faith based and inspirational stories, with a special focus on children 's books. My work explores family , spiritual growth , and emotional healing, often retelling biblical and historical stories with warmth , clarity , and heart . I aim to create meaningful stories that comfort, teach, and inspire readers of all ages .

Waiting for Dad (for every child who waited by the window)

Waiting for Dad is a heartfelt children's book about love, hope, and the quiet strength of a child waiting for a father who never comes. Told with honesty and tenderness, it gives a voice to children who feel unseen and reminds them they are never alone.